Focus on Earth Science

Minerals

Patricia Miller-Schroeder

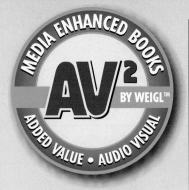

AV² provides enriched content that supplements and complements this book. Weigl's AV² books strive to create inspired learning and engage young minds in a total learning experience.

Your AV² Media Enhanced books come alive with...

 Audio
Listen to sections of the book read aloud.

Key Words
Study vocabulary, and complete a matching word activity.

 Video
Watch informative video clips.

 Quizzes
Test your knowledge.

 Embedded Weblinks
Gain additional information for research.

Slide Show
View images and captions, and prepare a presentation.

Try This!
Complete activities and hands-on experiments.

... and much, much more!

 Go to **www.av2books.com**, and enter this book's unique code.

BOOK CODE

B 236977

AV² by Weigl brings you media enhanced books that support active learning.

Published by AV² by Weigl
350 5th Avenue, 59th Floor
New York, NY 10118
Website: www.av2books.com

Library of Congress Control Number: 2015938071

ISBN 978-1-4896-4085-7 (hardcover)
ISBN 978-1-4896-4086-4 (softcover)
ISBN 978-1-4896-4087-1 (single user eBook)
ISBN 978-1-4896-4088-8 (multi-user eBook)

Printed in the United States of America in Brainerd, Minnesota
1 2 3 4 5 6 7 8 9 0 19 18 17 16 15

072015
170715

Project Coordinator Heather Kissock
Art Director Terry Paulhus

Photo Credits
Every reasonable effort has been made to trace ownership and to obtain permission to reprint copyright material. The publishers would be pleased to have any errors or omissions brought to their attention so that they may be corrected in subsequent printings.

Weigl acknowledges Getty Images, Alamy, and iStock as its primary image suppliers for this title.

Contents

Studying Minerals

Minerals are solid materials in nature that are not animals or plants. Scientists have found more than 3,000 types of minerals on Earth. Gold, copper, and iron are examples.

Minerals are everywhere. Table salt and beach sand are minerals. Cars, buses, and bicycles are made of minerals. There are even minerals in the human body. People's bodies have the greatest amounts of the minerals calcium and phosphorus. Minerals are the most common materials on Earth.

Minerals are found in space as well as on Earth. They are on other planets, on moons traveling around planets, and in **meteorites**. Some minerals are rare and expensive. Diamond is a mineral made of pure **carbon**. Carefully cut and polished diamonds are often used in wedding rings.

Pyrite is a mineral made of iron and sulfur. It is called "fool's gold" because it looks like gold but is not as valuable.

MORE ABOUT MINERALS

The first known use of the mineral turquoise dates back to **5000 BC** in Mesopotamia, a region in the Middle East.

Each person in the United States uses more than **48,000 pounds** (22,000 kilograms) of minerals every year.

One ounce (28 grams) of gold can be shaped into a thin wire **62 miles** (100 kilometers) long.

Diamonds are the **hardest** substance on Earth.

Scientists estimate that there are about **7,500 quadrillion** grains of sand in Earth's beaches and deserts.

Identifying Minerals

Scientists can often identify a mineral just by looking at a sample. Many minerals have rich colors, ranging from deep red to bright yellow. Green malachite and blue azurite are known by their colors. However, color is not always the best way to identify minerals. Some minerals can be found in several different colors.

There are many features that scientists use to help identify a mineral. These features are called properties. Luster is one property. Luster is the amount of shine a mineral has under a bright light. Some minerals, such as pyrite, shine brightly under light. Other minerals are dull.

Some minerals can be identified in other ways. Halite can be identified by taste. This mineral is commonly known as table salt. Other minerals have a distinct odor. Sulfur smells like rotten eggs.

Deposits of sulfur, salt, and other minerals can be found in the crater of a volcano in Dallol, Ethiopia.

STREAK COLORS OF DIFFERENT MINERALS

Streak is a property used to identify minerals. Streak is the color of the fine powder a mineral leaves when it is rubbed on a special tile. The color of the streak may be different from the mineral's color. However, the color of the streak is always the same for that mineral.

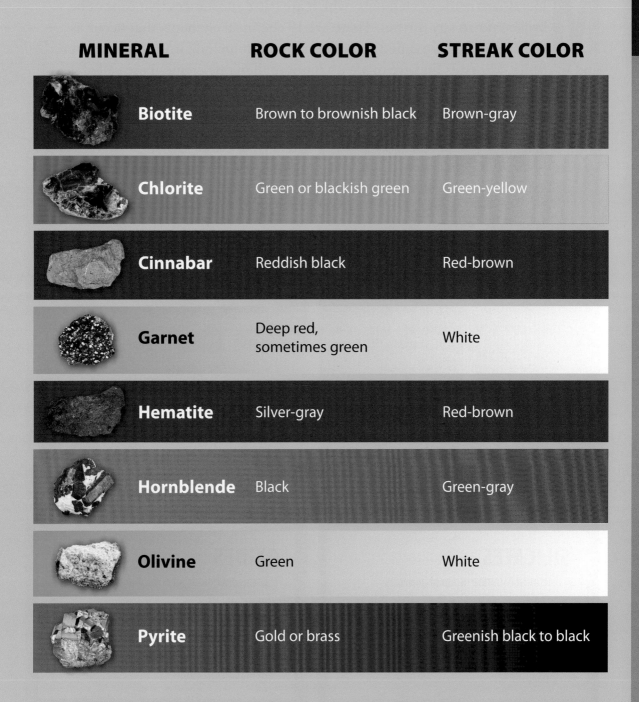

MINERAL	ROCK COLOR	STREAK COLOR
Biotite	Brown to brownish black	Brown-gray
Chlorite	Green or blackish green	Green-yellow
Cinnabar	Reddish black	Red-brown
Garnet	Deep red, sometimes green	White
Hematite	Silver-gray	Red-brown
Hornblende	Black	Green-gray
Olivine	Green	White
Pyrite	Gold or brass	Greenish black to black

Types of Minerals

Minerals are made of elements, which are basic substances that cannot be broken down any further. There are 19 chemical elements that occur as minerals. They are called native elements and include iron, silver, carbon, and **graphite**. Minerals that are made up of more than one element are called complex minerals. Minerals are grouped by their chemical makeup. The major mineral groups include silicates, oxides, carbonates, and sulfides.

TOPAZ

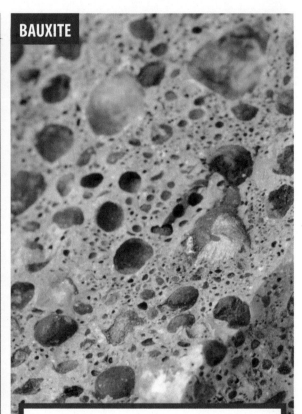

BAUXITE

SILICATES

- The most common group of minerals on Earth
- Created when metals mix with the elements silicon and oxygen
- Include mica, **quartz**, a gemstone called topaz, and talc

OXIDES

- Formed when oxygen combines with one or more metals
- Include the red gem ruby and the blue gem sapphire
- Bauxite, in the oxide mineral group, is used to make aluminum

ARAGONITE

CARBONATES

- A group of minerals made of carbon, oxygen, and a metal
- Include marble, aragonite, and calcite
- Calcite, one of Earth's most common minerals, comes in a variety of forms and colors

CINNABAR

SULFIDES

- Made of mixtures of sulfur and metals
- Are usually heavy and break easily
- Include arsenic, antimony, and cinnabar, which is used to make the mercury in thermometers

Crystals and Gemstones

Most minerals occur naturally as crystals. Crystals are solid substances with a pattern of flat surfaces called faces. Gemstones are minerals that have been cut and polished. They are often crystals with rich colors. The most valuable gemstones are also rare. Using a magnifying glass or **microscope** allows a person to view tiny crystals in gemstones or other minerals.

Advances in Mineralogy over Time

1700s

1735 Swedish scientist Carl Linnaeus publishes *System of Nature*, which divides the world into three kingdoms. They are animals, plants, and minerals.

1795 Scottish scientist James Hutton proposes a set of theories to explain the **geology** of Earth, including that all minerals and rocks began as fluids.

1791 Reverend William Gregor, an English chemist, first separates **titanium** from the mineral ilmenite. More than a century later, titanium will be important for making parts for airplanes and spacecraft.

1800s

1837 James Dana publishes *System of Mineralogy*, which is the basis for modern mineral classification.

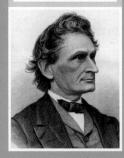

1882 Ellen Swallow Richards, the first woman admitted to the Massachusetts Institute of Technology, establishes the Women's Laboratory there. Courses included chemistry, biology, and mineralogy.

Each mineral has its own crystal pattern. This is as special as a person's fingerprints. No two minerals have the same pattern.

Scientists can tell what mineral they are looking at by examining its crystal pattern. Scientists have been studying crystals and other aspects of minerals for centuries. The study of minerals is called mineralogy.

Sharp crystals line the Cave of Crystals in northern Mexico. Scientists have been studying the formations since the cave was discovered in 2000.

1900s

2000s

1908 The Model T Ford becomes the first mass-produced car fueled by gasoline, made from the mineral petroleum. Mass-production means manufactured in large numbers using machinery.

1954 Scientists at Bell Labs make the first silicon transistor, a small electrical switch that is the foundation of modern computers and other electronics products.

2015 After more than 10 years in space, the National Aeronautics and Space Administration's *Messenger* spacecraft runs out of fuel and crashes into the planet Mercury. Measurements and images collected by the spacecraft are helping scientists identify minerals in Mercury's crust.

1951 Uranium, found in several minerals, is used for the first time to produce electricity when a nuclear plant in Arco, Idaho, powers four light bulbs.

MINERALS
around the World

ARCTIC
OCEAN

Pb **Ni** **Ag**
Zn **U**

Canada

NORTH
AMERICA

Name: Peñasquito Silver Mine
Continent: North America
Location: Zacatecas, Mexico
Fast Fact: The world's largest silver mine has enough of this mineral to operate until 2035.

Pb **Ag** **P**
Cu **Zn** **U**

United States

ATLANTIC
OCEAN

Ag **Zn** ← Mexico

PACIFIC
OCEAN

Cu **Au**
Ag **Sn**

Peru

SOUTH
AMERICA

Brazil →

Al **Ni**
Sn **U**

Cu ← Chile

Legend

N ↑

620 Miles
0   1,000 Kilometers

Al Aluminum		**Pt** Platinum	
Cu Copper		**Ag** Silver	
Au Gold		**Sn** Tin	
Pb Lead		**U** Uranium	
Ni Nickel		**Zn** Zinc	
P Phosphorus			

Name: Escondida Copper Mine
Continent: South America
Location: Atacama Desert, Chile
Fast Fact: This mine has produced as much as 1.3 million tons (1.2 million metric tons) of copper per year.

FIND OUT MORE ABOUT MINERALS

This map shows the location of certain minerals around the world, as well as important mineral sites. Use this map, and research online to answer these questions.

1. Which country is the largest producer of each mineral?
2. Where is the mineral phosphorus found? What is it used for?

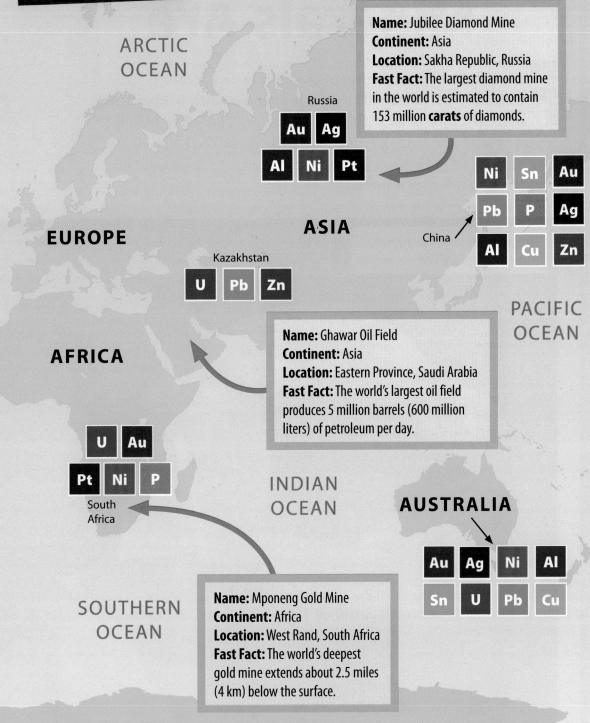

ARCTIC OCEAN

Name: Jubilee Diamond Mine
Continent: Asia
Location: Sakha Republic, Russia
Fast Fact: The largest diamond mine in the world is estimated to contain 153 million **carats** of diamonds.

Russia

Au   Ag
Al   Ni   Pt

EUROPE

ASIA

China

Ni   Sn   Au
Pb   P   Ag
Al   Cu   Zn

Kazakhstan

U   Pb   Zn

Name: Ghawar Oil Field
Continent: Asia
Location: Eastern Province, Saudi Arabia
Fast Fact: The world's largest oil field produces 5 million barrels (600 million liters) of petroleum per day.

PACIFIC OCEAN

AFRICA

U   Au
Pt   Ni   P

South Africa

INDIAN OCEAN

AUSTRALIA

Au   Ag   Ni   Al
Sn   U   Pb   Cu

SOUTHERN OCEAN

Name: Mponeng Gold Mine
Continent: Africa
Location: West Rand, South Africa
Fast Fact: The world's deepest gold mine extends about 2.5 miles (4 km) below the surface.

ANTARCTICA

Measuring How Hard Minerals Are

Friedrich Mohs was a German scientist who lived from 1773 to 1839. In 1801, he moved to Austria after a wealthy banker hired him to study a valuable mineral collection. This job led Mohs to invent in 1812 a scale to describe the hardness of different minerals. The Mohs Scale of Hardness is widely used today by scientists and people who work with minerals.

Some minerals, such as quartz, will scratch other minerals, such as calcite.

Some minerals are much harder than others. The scale ranks minerals in order of hardness from one for softest to ten for hardest. Mohs rated minerals by testing which ones could scratch others. Minerals that are low on the scale can be scratched easily, even with a fingernail. Minerals high on the scale are difficult to scratch, even with a **file**. Diamonds have a hardness of ten. They cannot be scratched by any other mineral.

MOHS SCALE OF HARDNESS

Mohs used ten common minerals to develop his scale.

10 Diamond	Scratches all other minerals
9 Corundum	Cuts glass, which is made up largely of quartz
8 Topaz	Scratches glass easily
7 Quartz	Is not scratched by a file
6 Feldspar	Cannot be scratched with a knife
5 Apatite	Is scratched with a knife with difficulty
4 Fluorite	Is not scratched by a copper coin and does not scratch glass
3 Calcite	Scratches and is scratched by a copper coin
2 Gypsum	Is scratched with difficulty by a fingernail
1 Talc	Is easily scratched by a fingernail

Common Uses of Minerals

Minerals are used to make parts of many everyday objects. Quartz is one of the most common minerals. Besides being used to make glass, quartz is used for watch parts, electronic equipment, and many other products.

Gypsum is another common mineral. It is used in cement, toothpaste, crayons, and bakery products. Copper is used to make coins, electrical wire, pipes, and airbags in automobiles. Diamonds have many uses because of their hardness. They are valuable in drill bits, saws, and other cutting tools. The small straight knives called scalpels that are used by doctors for surgery often have diamond blades.

The mineral gypsum is used in drywall, or panels that cover the inside walls and ceilings of buildings. Drywall is sometimes called gypsum board.

The bodies of humans and animals need a certain amount of halite, or salt, to stay healthy. Today and in the past, people use salt to flavor food and also to preserve it, or keep it from spoiling. Some salt is mined from salt flats, or the salt-covered bottoms of dried up lakes. Many types of animals use **salt licks** to take in halite. Through history, salt has been used as a form of money. Soldiers were paid with salt in Ancient Rome, where people spoke Latin. The Latin word *salarium* meant "salt money." It is the origin of the English word *salary*.

4,085
Square Miles
The size of Uyuni in Bolivia, the world's largest salt flat.
(10,580 sq. km)

25,000
TONS
The weight of the salt taken from Uyuni Salt Flat every year.
(22,700 metric tons)

10
BILLION TONS
The estimated amount of remaining salt in Uyuni Salt Flat.
(9 billion metric tons)

The Myth of Amethyst

In the past, people created stories to explain the world around them. These stories are called myths. Many myths are from Ancient Greece. One of these myths describes how the gem amethyst was created.

Dionysus, the Ancient Greek god of wine, was angry one day. He decided to have his tigers eat the next person to walk by him. That person was a young woman named Amethyst. In order to save the young woman, Artemis, the goddess of nature, animals, and the hunt, turned her into a white stone. Then, Dionysus felt sorry about what had happened. He poured wine over the white stone, turning it a shade of purple. That is how the mineral amethyst got its color and name.

Amethyst is a variety of quartz.

What Is a Mineralogist?

People who study rocks and minerals are called mineralogists. These scientists try to learn where minerals are found and how they form. They identify different minerals by studying their properties. Mineralogists work for governments, universities, and research organizations. Mining companies also use these experts. Some mineralogists study minerals from space.

Tools

Mineralogists use powerful **electron** microscopes and **X-rays**. They use these tools to see the inner structure of minerals. They look at minerals with magnifying lenses. A collection bag holds samples picked up in nature to be carried back to the laboratory.

Safety

Mineralogists often work outdoors. Research trips can take them to remote areas with harsh climates. Mineralogists who work with harmful materials must take special care.

Mineralogists use special hammers and picks to remove minerals from rocky areas for further study.

Mineral Work

7,900
There are this many mining and geological engineers working in the United States.

42%
This portion of mineralogists have bachelor's and master's degrees.

1919
This is the year that the professional group Mineralogical Society of America was founded.

Minerals Quiz

Now that you have read all about minerals, test your knowledge by answering these questions. All of the information can be found in the text you just read. The answers are provided below for easy reference.

1 How many grains of sand do scientists estimate are in Earth's beaches and deserts?

4 What does the Mohs scale measure?

7 What is the hardest substance on Earth?

2 What does the mineral sulfur smell like?

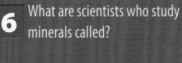

3 What is pyrite sometimes called?

5 What is the streak color of hematite?

6 What are scientists who study minerals called?

8 In which country is the largest salt flat on Earth found?

9 How many pounds of minerals does each person in the United States use every year?

10 What are four products that copper is used to make?

Science in Action

Crystals form in several ways. You can see how simple crystals form using water, a string, and some sugar.

BEFORE YOU START, YOU WILL NEED:

A piece of string

A glass

A pencil

A spoon

Sugar

Water

Food coloring

Growing Crystals

1 Tie a piece of string that is slightly shorter than the glass to the middle of the pencil.

2 With an adult's help, boil some water.

3 Dissolve several spoonfuls of sugar in the hot water. Add a few drops of food coloring to the water, and stir.

4 With the adult's help, fill the glass with hot water containing the sugar and food coloring.

5 Lay the pencil across the top of the glass so that the string is dangling inside the glass. Make sure the string does not touch the sides or bottom of the glass.

6 Put the glass in a safe place where it will not be moved. Check it every day for a few days. As the sugar water cools, sugar crystals will begin to form on the string. Layers of crystals will build up and continue to grow for a time. When the crystals seem to have stopped growing, pull the string out of the water, let it dry, and observe your crystals.

Key Words

carats: units of weight for precious stones equal to 0.007 ounces (200 milligrams)

carbon: a chemical element found in coal, diamonds, and all plants and animals

electron: a tiny particle that moves around the nucleus, or center, of an atom

file: a metal tool with ridges used to cut, smooth, or grind hard surfaces

geology: the study of Earth's layers of soil and rock

graphite: a dark, soft mineral used in pencils, in batteries, and for certain parts of electric motors

meteorites: rocks traveling in space that fall to Earth's surface

microscope: a device used to make very small objects appear larger, so that they can be seen and studied

quartz: a hard mineral that appears in many colors and forms

salt licks: natural deposits of salt that animals, such as deer and sheep, regularly lick to stay healthy

titanium: a very strong metal

X-rays: invisible high-energy rays that pass through objects and are used for making images

Index

Log on to www.av2books.com

AV² by Weigl brings you media enhanced books that support active learning. Go to www.av2books.com, and enter the special code found on page 2 of this book. You will gain access to enriched and enhanced content that supplements and complements this book. Content includes video, audio, weblinks, quizzes, a slide show, and activities.

AV² Online Navigation

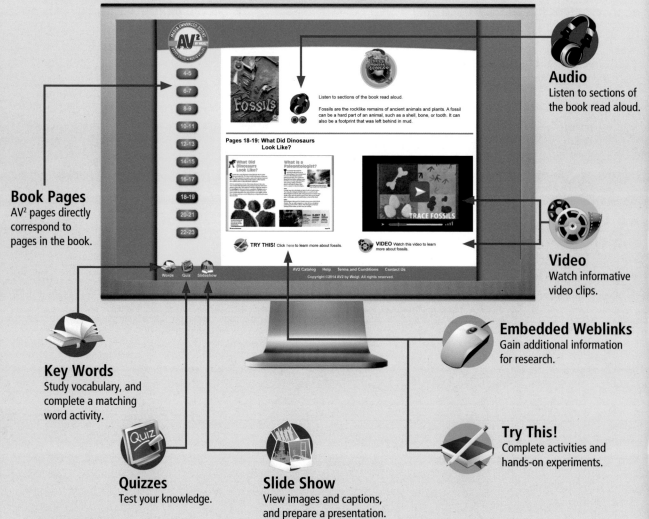

Audio
Listen to sections of the book read aloud.

Video
Watch informative video clips.

Embedded Weblinks
Gain additional information for research.

Try This!
Complete activities and hands-on experiments.

Book Pages
AV² pages directly correspond to pages in the book.

Key Words
Study vocabulary, and complete a matching word activity.

Quizzes
Test your knowledge.

Slide Show
View images and captions, and prepare a presentation.

AV² was built to bridge the gap between print and digital. We encourage you to tell us what you like and what you want to see in the future.

Sign up to be an AV² Ambassador at www.av2books.com/ambassador.

Due to the dynamic nature of the Internet, some of the URLs and activities provided as part of AV² by Weigl may have changed or ceased to exist. AV² by Weigl accepts no responsibility for any such changes. All media enhanced books are regularly monitored to update addresses and sites in a timely manner. Contact AV² by Weigl at 1-866-649-3445 or av2books@weigl.com with any questions, comments, or feedback.